HEADLINE ISSUES

Getting Rid of Waste

Angela Royston

www.heinemannlibrary.co.uk
Visit our website to find out more information about **Heinemann Library** books.

To order:
☎ Phone 44 (0) 1865 888066
▤ Send a fax to 44 (0) 1865 314091
▣ Visit the Heinemann Bookshop at www.heinemannlibrary.co.uk to browse our catalogue and order online.

Heinemann Library is an imprint of Capstone Global Library Limited, a company incorporated in England and Wales having its registered office at 7 Pilgrim Street, London, EC4V 6LB - Registered company number: 6695582

"Heinemann" is a registered trademark of Pearson Education Limited, under licence to Capstone Global Library Limited

Text © Capstone Global Library Limited 2009
First published in hardback in 2009
The moral rights of the proprietor have been asserted.

Edited by Sarah Eason and Leon Gray
Designed by Calcium and Geoff Ward
Original illustrations © Capstone Global Library Limited 2009
Illustrated by Geoff Ward
Picture research by Maria Joannou
Originated by Heinemann Library
Printed and bound in China by CTPS

ISBN 978 0 431162 71 3 (hardback)
13 12 11 10 09
10 9 8 7 6 5 4 3 2 1

British Library Cataloguing in Publication Data
Royston, Angela
    Getting rid of waste. - (Headline issues)
    1. Refuse and refuse disposal - Juvenile literature 2. Recycling (Waste, etc.) - Juvenile literature
    I. Title
    363.7'28
A full catalogue record for this book is available from the British Library.

Acknowledgements
We would like to thank the following for permission to reproduce photographs:
Alamy Images: Grant Heilman Photography/Larry Lefever 24, JL Jahn 19b; Corbis: Patrick Bennett 5b, Zhou Chao/EPA 15b, Paul A. Souders 12, Jose Manuel Vidal/EPA 5t; Dreamstime: Stephen Finn 3, 22–23; FLPA: Rosemary Mayer 25; Fotolia: Bilderbox 15t; Getty Images: Justin Sullivan 6; Istockphoto: Marissa Childs 10, Ernesto Solla Domínguez 7, Bojan Fatur 30–31, Steve Geer 11, Nemanja Glumac 8–9, Sebastian Hosche 4–5, Jim Jurica 32, Roman Milert 21t, David Orr 20–21, Christian Riedel 16, Edward Shaw 24–25; PA Photos: Toby Melville/PA Archive 17; Rex Features: 26; Science Photo Library: Erika Craddock 9b, Sheila Terry 19t; Shutterstock: 6–7, 16–17, 18–19, Imageshunter 10–11, Chris Jenner 9t, Dejan Lazarevic 12–13, Isakov Eduard Olegovich 23b, Prism 68 28–29, 29, Radu Razvan 27, Aida Ricciardiello 1, 20, Sally Scott 23t, Roman Sigaev 21b, Marek Slusarczyk 13, Makarov Vladyslav 28, Michael Zysman 14–15.

Cover photograph reproduced with permission of Rex Features/Nick Cunard.

Every effort has been made to contact copyright holders of material reproduced in this book. Any omissions will be rectified in subsequent printings if notice is given to the publishers.

Disclaimer

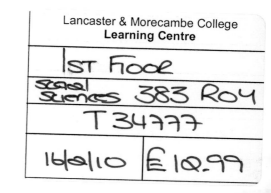

12.99

1 MAR 2018

Return on or before the last date stamped above.

Author - ROYSTON, Angela

Title - GETTING RID OF WASTE

Class Number - 383 ROY   **T Number -** T34777

Contents

Some words are printed in bold, **like this**. You can find out what they mean by looking in the glossary on page 30.

Rubbish piles up

PEOPLE WHO LIVE in rich countries produce enormous amounts of rubbish every year. It is easy to throw away empty plastic cartons, metal cans, scrap paper, and other items when we have finished with them. We put them in a rubbish bag and dump them in the bin. Every week a dustbin lorry comes and empties the bin. The waste is then taken away. That is the last we usually see of our rubbish.

What's in the rubbish?

Most of our household rubbish consists of cardboard, scraps of paper, and plastic waste. The rest is mainly food waste, glass, and metal cans. People also throw away larger items they no longer want, such as computers, refrigerators, and furniture.

Some rubbish breaks down very quickly. For example, scraps of food break down in the soil, making it easier for plants to grow.

Other rubbish, such as glass, takes thousands of years to break down. In 2003, **archaeologists** found the remains of an ancient glass-making factory at Qantir in Egypt. There they found glass beads and fragments from bottles and other items dating from about 2500 BCE.

Getting rid of rubbish

In most countries, the **local council** collects the rubbish. They organize dustbin lorries to come to our houses, empty our bins, and take away the rubbish.

Most of this rubbish ends up at a **landfill site**. There it is buried in the ground and left to rot away. The problem is that local councils are running out of landfill sites. We do not have enough land left to fill with rubbish. Councils need to find better ways of dealing with all the rubbish. Most importantly, they need to encourage people to start **recycling** and reduce the amount of waste they produce.

FACT!

✦ Every household in Britain produces about 1 tonne (1.1 tons) of rubbish every year.
✦ Households in Australia and the United States produce even more rubbish.
✦ About 30 per cent of all household rubbish is **packaging**.

ON THE SPOT
Naples

Rubbish piles up in Naples

It's March 2008, and bags of rubbish are piled high in the streets of Naples in Italy. The landfill sites are full, and there is nowhere else to put it. The people of Naples are so angry that they set fire to the rubbish. The piles soon start to build up again.

Bags of rubbish pile high in Naples. This is a serious health risk to the people of the city.

A dustbin lorry collects household rubbish from a street in Australia.

Too much packaging

M OST OF THE things we buy have too much **packaging**. Packaging makes things easier for the shops to handle and sell. All this packaging puts up the price of items sold. Packaging can make things look more attractive, but it all ends up in the bin.

Unnecessary packaging

Many items have unnecessary packaging. Computer games and DVDs usually come in strong, plastic boxes. The boxes are much bigger than the disks themselves. Sometimes computer games and DVDs are given away free with newspapers and magazines. Then the only packaging is a sleeve made of thin card. This shows that the plastic boxes are unnecessary.

Protective wrapping

Many items need some packaging. A computer contains many parts that are kept together in one box. The box also protects the computer from being scratched and damaged during **transit** between the factory and your home.

Food is put into packaging to protect it and keep it clean. Almost everything is packaged in supermarkets, from meat and fish to fruit and vegetables. In farm shops and markets, however, most food items are sold without all this packaging. Do we really need it?

Part of the price of DVDs and Blu-ray discs is to cover the cost of packaging. Which would you prefer? A higher price or less packaging?

Packaging is unnecessary: Who is right and who is wrong?

FOR

One example of unnecessary packaging is when supermarkets sell apples on specially shaped plastic trays. If other apples can be sold loose, why can't they all? Cucumbers already have a skin, so why do they need to be **shrink-wrapped** as well? A tube of toothpaste doesn't need to be inside a cardboard box.

These apples are packed in plastic trays to protect them. This extra packaging will end up in the bin.

AGAINST

Packaging is needed to protect food and other items from damage. Shrink-wrapping keeps cucumbers fresher for longer. Plastic trays stop apples from becoming bruised. Similarly, a cardboard box protects the tube of toothpaste from being squeezed and damaged.

The plastic problem – it won't go away

Plastic is so cheap that it is used to make almost everything. Plastic is cheaper and lighter than many other materials, but it does not rot. Plastic is also made from oil taken from the ground. Oil is an extremely valuable resource that should not be wasted on unnecessary plastic **packaging**.

No one knows how long plastic lasts, because people have only been making it for around 150 years. The plastic you throw away today will probably still be in the **landfill site** in 500 years.

Plastic bottles

Most liquids, from fresh milk to motor oil, are sold in plastic bottles. Bottled water has become very popular in the last ten years. Most people usually throw the bottle away when they have finished it.

All these empty water bottles are then put into rubbish bins and end up in landfill sites. Many plastic bottles find their way into rivers and are washed out to sea.

Plastic bags

Plastic bags are so cheap that shops often give them away. When you buy some groceries or a new T-shirt, for example, you probably take them home in a plastic bag. Plastic bags make it easy to carry things but they add to the rubbish in our bins. They also blow through the streets, clog up drains, and get stuck in trees.

In many countries, you have to pay for all the plastic bags you use. In 2002, Bangladesh became the first country to ban plastic shopping bags. Many other countries have followed suit.

FACT!

✦ In the United States, 29 billion plastic water bottles are thrown away each year.
✦ Transporting bottles of water from factories to shops adds to traffic pollution.
✦ Filling an empty bottle with tap water is 500 times cheaper than buying bottled water.

Since fast-food sellers in Taiwan were banned from using plastic cups, plates, and cutlery, the amount of rubbish sent to landfill sites has dropped by 25 per cent.

ON THE SPOT
Modbury, Devon

Modbury

You won't be welcome in Modbury in Devon, England, if you are carrying a plastic bag! In April 2007, the townspeople and shopkeepers got together and agreed never to use plastic bags again. Now local people take their own cloth bags and baskets whenever they go shopping.

The people of Modbury carry their shopping in reusable cloth bags.

Rivers of rubbish

MANY RIVERS ARE becoming huge drains that carry unwanted waste into the oceans. Some people dump rubbish straight into **canals** and rivers. Cans, paper, and plastic **litter** float on the water. Sometimes shopping trolleys and old cars are pushed into canals, too. However, litter is not the only problem. **Sewage** and waste from factories and buildings also **pollute** many rivers.

Dying river
The Yangtze River flows across China. It is the third longest river in the world – and one of the most polluted. Almost 200 cities rely on the water for drinking, cleaning, and other uses.

For centuries, people have eaten fish caught in the Yangtze River. However, the fish and animals that live along the banks of the river are dying out. They are being poisoned by waste from farms and cities.

Poisonous pollution
Most farmers spray their crops with chemicals called pesticides. The farmers use these chemicals to kill insects and other pests that damage the crops. Some pesticides wash into the Yangtze River. Factories and cities pour dirty water into the river. The river is so big, and the water flows so fast, that the pollution is washed out to sea. However, the water in the river is slowly getting dirty. The fish are struggling to survive.

These swans are fighting over a piece of plastic. If either swallows the plastic, it could choke on it and die.

BEHIND THE HEADLINES
Coming back to life

The River Thames in London, England, used to be much dirtier than the Yangtze River is today. Fifty years ago, no fish swam in it. If someone fell into the Thames, they were in serious danger of dying from swallowing the dirty water.

Since then, new laws have been passed to clean up the river. Sewage and waste water from factories must be cleaned before it can drain into the water. The River Thames is now much cleaner than before.

Now the water is much cleaner, many kinds of fish are swimming in the River Thames.

Plastic ocean soup

Countless tiny pieces of plastic are floating around the Pacific Ocean. The plastic covers an area much bigger than the land surface area of the United States. This floating "plastic continent" includes crates and other large pieces of plastic waste. It also includes broken cups, bottles, small pieces of plastic bags, and even used toothbrushes. This waste forms a kind of plastic soup in the ocean.

Dumping rubbish

All this plastic waste was thrown away by **developed countries** such as Britain, China, France, and the United States. Some of it was thrown into rivers and washed into the oceans. About 20 per cent of the rubbish was thrown from ships and oil platforms. Sea birds, fish, and other sea creatures think the plastic is food. They eat the plastic items by mistake. Poisons in the plastic then build up in the fish. When people or other animals eat the fish, they are eating the poisons, too.

Floating yellow ducks

In 1992, a **container ship** was caught in a storm in the Pacific Ocean. Some of its **cargo** was washed into the sea, including about 30,000 plastic bath toys. Ten months later, plastic ducks began to wash up on the west coast of Canada. More than ten years later, plastic ducks were still being washed ashore in New England on the east coast of the United States. To get there they must have floated right around the north of Canada!

People should not litter the oceans with old fishing nets because seals and other sea creatures can get caught and be choked by them.

BEHIND THE HEADLINES
Ocean currents

Ocean **currents** are like rivers in the sea. Currents in the Pacific Ocean sweep around in a huge circle. The currents are collectively known as the Pacific Gyre. The Pacific Gyre carries litter from both sides of the Pacific into the middle of the ocean. There, the litter floats just below the surface. Some of it washes up on to the coasts of the Hawaiian Islands. Some of it has been floating round the oceans for more than 50 years.

Plastic does not rot, so all the waste in the world's oceans is becoming a big problem.

Filling the land with rubbish

In just one year, all the people of the United States produce enough rubbish to fill a hole the same size as a football pitch and 160 kilometres (100 miles) deep.

In fact, most countries do bury their rubbish, but not all in one place. They bury it in old **quarries** and specially dug holes called **landfill sites**. However, landfill sites cause many problems for the environment and for the people who live near them.

Fresh Kills

One of the biggest rubbish dumps in the world can be found on Staten Island in New York City. The Fresh Kills landfill site is so huge that you can even see it from space. It measures 70 metres (225 feet) at its highest point and covers around 880 hectares (2,200 acres).

The site received all the rubbish from New York City for more than 50 years, but it has since been sealed up. There are plans to turn the area into a park.

No one likes living next to a rubbish dump. Most landfill sites are ugly and smelly. The rubbish attracts rats. Poisonous liquids and gases seep out of the rotting rubbish. The waste liquids leak into the soil and nearby rivers and poison them, too.

Modern landfill sites

Engineers have tried to solve some of these problems. Modern sites have a waterproof lining to stop waste liquids from leaking out. The gases given off by the rubbish, such as **methane**, are collected and burned to **generate** electricity for local people.

FACT!

✦ Americans produce almost twice as much rubbish as people in other **developed countries**.
✦ Greece buries more rubbish in landfill sites than any other European country.
✦ Britain will run out of landfill sites by 2016.

Landfill sites contain all kinds of rubbish, including glass, metals, wood, and other items that can be sold.

ON THE SPOT
Manila

Manila

Thousands of poor families live on landfill sites in Manila in the Philippines. They search the sites for rubbish they can use or sell. They find clothes, bedding, and materials to build their homes. The children help to sort through the rubbish. Living on a dump is very dangerous and unhealthy, but millions of the world's poorest people still live on dumps in **developing countries**.

Dump dwellers in Manila in the Philippines make a living by searching through the rubbish, looking for things they can sell.

A burning issue

In July 2007, residents in Kuala Lumpur in Malaysia were celebrating. They were happy because the government had scrapped a plan to build one of the world's largest **incinerators** in their neighbourhood.

Incinerators are huge **furnaces** that burn rubbish. Some people say that incinerators are the best way to solve the problems of **landfill sites**. So why do local people often oppose them?

Burning rubbish

Incinerators can burn a lot of rubbish. The incinerator in Kuala Lumpur was designed to burn nearly 1,500 tonnes (1,665 tons) a day. Some incinerators use the heat from the burning rubbish to **generate** electricity. Modern incinerators heat the rubbish so much that it turns into a gas. This gas is then burned to generate electricity.

Poisonous gases

Burning rubbish produces toxic gases. The gases contain chemicals that cause **cancer** and other illnesses. This is the main reason why people do not want incinerators near where they live. However, the gases can also be blown in the wind and harm people hundreds of kilometres away. When the rubbish has burned, it leaves behind ash. The ash contains toxic chemicals, too. If it is buried in landfill, the ash poisons the soil.

This incinerator in Vienna in Austria makes electricity. Tourists come to see the building, which was decorated by an artist.

Burning rubbish is safe:
Who is right and who is wrong?

FOR

Burying rubbish in the ground takes up too much space. We need to burn it to get rid of it. Using rubbish to generate electricity saves burning oil and natural gas. Modern incinerators stop most of the poisonous gases from getting into the air.

People in Edmonton in London, England, held a protest on top of an incinerator to stop a similar one from being built in their neighbourhood.

AGAINST

Stopping poisonous gases escaping into the air is good, but it makes the ash even more toxic. The best way to solve the problem is by producing less in the first place, which means more **recycling**.

Greatest recyclers of the world

RECYCLING KEEPS RUBBISH out of **landfill sites** and **incinerators**. Cardboard, glass, paper, metal, and some types of plastic can be recycled and used again and again.

World leaders

In Switzerland, people recycle more than 90 per cent of their waste glass. This is more than any other country. Japan tops the league when it comes to recycling steel cans. It recycles nearly 90 per cent of them. Australians lead the world when it comes to recycling newspapers. They recycle about 75 per cent of their newspapers.

Making recycling work

The Netherlands recycles almost 70 per cent of all the waste that it produces. This is more than any other **developed country** in the world. **Local councils** provide the people with special bins.

Different bins are used to collect different kinds of waste.

In Germany, 90 per cent of people sort out their rubbish into five different recycling bins. The Germans claim that this makes them the recycling champions of the world!

Expert recyclers

People in many **developing countries** do not need recycling bins. They are already experts at recycling. They reuse and recycle almost everything. For example, newspapers are used to make wrapping paper, and empty containers are used as cups.

Even orange peel is collected in Senegal – a developing nation in West Africa. People use the oils from the orange peel to make a fragrant perfume.

FACT!

✦ Recycling 1 tonne (1.1 tons) of paper saves 30,000 litres (63,000 pints) of water.
✦ It also saves as much electricity as an average home in Britain uses in one year.

BEHIND THE HEADLINES

Beyond the recycling centre

The materials that are collected for recycling are sent to a transit centre. There they are cleaned, sorted, and bundled up before they are sent for **processing**. For example, paper is sent to a **paper mill**, where it is pulped and made into new paper. Recycled paper is used mainly for printing newspapers. It can also be used for greetings cards, tissues, and office paper.

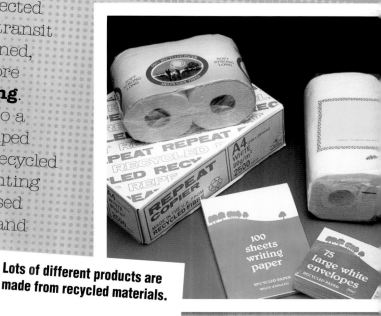

Lots of different products are made from recycled materials.

A recycling centre does not look very glamorous, but it does a vital job. Recycling rubbish saves it from being incinerated or buried in a landfill site.

Fast-track recycling

THE DRINKS CANS you put into the **recycling** bin are **processed** and made into new drinks cans. The process is so fast that the recycled cans can be in the shops just six weeks after putting them into the recycling bin.

Most drinks cans are made from **aluminium**. Food cans are made from steel. Using recycled aluminium and steel saves electricity. This means that it is much cheaper than making cans from new aluminium or steel.

Recycling metal

Drinks and food cans are collected in the same recycling bin. **Magnets** are used to separate the steel from the aluminium. Steel is attracted to a magnet but aluminium is not. The cans are then sent to be processed.

The aluminium cans are hammered by a machine into small pieces.

The metal pieces are heated in an incredibly hot oven until they melt. When the aluminium cools, it is rolled into thin sheets. Some of the sheets are made into drinks cans. Other sheets are made even thinner and used for aluminium foil. Steel cans are melted in much the same way as the aluminium ones and made into blocks of steel.

Recycling glass

Glass is one of the easiest materials to recycle. Clear, green, and brown glass is collected in separate recycling bins. Clear glass is melted and made into new clear glass bottles and jars. Brown and green glass is also melted and made into new glass of the same colour.

Recycling paper

Recycling old newspapers and other paper waste saves the environment. It means that fewer trees are cut down to make new paper.

FACT!

◆ Recycling aluminium saves 90 per cent of the electricity needed to make new aluminium.
◆ Recycling one glass bottle saves enough electricity to power an electric light for four hours. Cleaning the bottle and reusing it saves even more!

Most drinks cans are made from aluminium. It costs a lot of money to make this metal. It is much cheaper to recycle aluminium.

ON THE SPOT
Britain

Many roads in Britain are built using crushed green glass. Britain collects more bottles made from green glass than it can recycle as new bottles. Some of the glass is crushed so finely that it looks like sand. This is then used to build the roads.

Glass bottles can be green, brown, or clear. All of them can be recycled.

Once a plastic bottle, now what?

PLASTIC DRINKS BOTTLES should always be recycled. They can be used to make many different things. For example, they can become a new plastic bottle, a CD case, or even a warm fleece.

Drinks bottles

At the **processing** plant, clear plastic drinks bottles are washed and chopped into small pieces. The plastic pieces are melted and cooled to form beads or a fine thread.

The plastic beads are melted and made into new bottles. Some of the thread is used to weave carpets and make fleeces, scarfs, and gloves. Some of the thread is spun into a fluffy mass that looks a bit like candy floss. This is used as the lining for sleeping bags. The mass of fluffy thread traps air, which keeps you warm while you are sleeping at night.

Milk bottles

Shampoo bottles and other bottles made of **translucent** plastic are recycled along with milk bottles. They are processed in the same way as the clear plastic and made into beads. The only difference is that the plastic beads are black.

The black beads are sent to factories where they are melted and made into toys, plant pots, rubbish bags, and other useful items. Some of the black plastic beads are also made into drain pipes.

Saving energy

Milk and other drinks were once sold in glass bottles. After use, the empty bottles were collected, cleaned, and reused. Many were reused more than 50 times before they got broken. This reduced waste and saved energy making new bottles.

FACT!

◆ Between one and two out of every ten plastic bottles are recycled around the world.
◆ Just 25 2-litre (4.25 pint) drinks bottles are all that is needed to make one fleece.
◆ Around 30 per cent of all plastic is used as packaging.

BEHIND THE HEADLINES
Plastic

There are about 50 different types of plastic. All types of plastic can be recycled, but each one has to be processed separately. Most **local councils** are not willing to sort out the different plastics and send them for reprocessing. Usually recycling centres accept only plastic bottles.

This black flower pot was made from recycled plastic milk bottles. You can also plant flowers in reused plastic yoghurt pots.

Plastic thread was used to weave these fleece gloves. It was made from recycled plastic bottles.

Compost it

INSTEAD OF THROWING food scraps and peelings into the bin, you can save them to make **compost**. Compost is a kind of soil that is good for growing plants. This is because it is full of nutrients. Waste food, leaves, and all kinds of **organic** material slowly rot and turn into compost. Many **local councils** collect scrap food and garden waste to make compost. They use it in parks and gardens to help plants grow better.

Compost bins

If your council does not recycle food and garden waste, you can use it to make your own compost. If you are going to use scraps of food, it is best to use a special composting bin. This will prevent rats and other pests from causing a problem.

Microbes, insects, and worms break down the food and garden waste. Some things break down quicker than others. You can buy special chemicals to make the waste break down faster.

Sewage

All the dirty water from baths, factories, sinks, and toilets is called **sewage**. This sewage goes down the drain. It ends up in large pipes that carry the waste water to a sewage works. There the dirty water is filtered and cleaned. The clean water is then pumped back into rivers and streams. The sludge left behind at the sewage works can be turned into compost.

Many gardeners pile up dead leaves and other plant matter to make compost. They use this to fertilize the soil, helping new plants to grow.

BEHIND THE HEADLINES
Wormery

Worms love kitchen waste. A **wormery** is a special bin. It has several layers and lots of worms. Waste fruit and vegetables, tea bags, and other food scraps go into the top of the bin. The worms then get to work eating the scraps. As the food breaks down, it falls through the layers. Eventually it becomes a liquid compost, which collects at the bottom of the compost bin. The liquid is drained off and used as a plant feed. The compost is added to soil in plant pots and flower beds.

A wormery is a living compost bin. Worms eat the food scraps to make the compost.

Pass it on

W E SHOULD ALL reduce the amount of rubbish we produce. The best way is to avoid buying new things.

When something wears out or breaks down, try to repair it. Think of ways of reusing things that you no longer need. For example, you could also pass on unwanted items, such as clothes, to somebody who might find them useful.

Repair

In the past, people used to mend worn shoes and clothes. When something breaks down today, most people buy a new item to replace it. Manufacturers make things so that they wear out after a short time. They want people to buy new things.

Reuse

People in **developing countries** waste very little. They collect items made from glass, metal, and other materials and sell them. Many people in the developed world are starting to reuse items that they no longer need.

When you have grown out of clothes, it is a good idea to give them to a **charity shop**. Charity shops are also good places to buy clothes, books, toys, and other items. Some people hold car boot sales or post items on auction sites on the Internet. You will be amazed at what you can sell, so sort out your junk and pass it on!

You can buy cheap clothes in a second-hand clothes shop. Some of the clothes have hardly been worn.

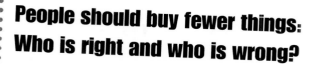

People should buy fewer things: Who is right and who is wrong?

FOR

People waste a lot of the stuff that they buy. Most people have to throw away food because they did not eat it before it went bad. Others buy clothes they hardly wear. If people had to pay more, they would only buy the things they really want.

AGAINST

Many items, such as computers and mobile phones, are getting better all the time. People buy new things to keep up with the latest technologies. Lots of people work in factories that make things. If we bought fewer things, some of them would lose their jobs.

Many people make money and reduce waste by selling things they don't need at jumble sales.

Get involved!

There is a lot that you and your family can do to reduce how much rubbish you throw away. All you have to do is to follow the four "Rs" below: reduce, repair, reuse, and **recycle**.

The four "Rs"

Reduce
- Buy fewer things. Only buy things you need and you know you will use.

Repair
- When a machine breaks down, see if someone can repair it.
- If your shoes wear out, see if they can be fixed.
- If an item of clothing becomes torn, see if it can be mended.

Reuse
- Think about how you can reuse empty yoghurt pots and other containers. You might use them as plant pots or to store leftover food. Empty boxes and tins could make handy jewellery boxes.
- Take clothes, books, toys, and other items you no longer want to a **charity shop**. They will sell them and use the money to help people in need.
- Provided your old computer is still working, find out if there is a charity or company near you that will take it and pass it on to someone else.
- Save **giftwrap** and reuse it.

If you see this logo on something, it means you can recycle it after you have used it.

Clean and squash plastic bottles flat before you recycle them.

Recycle

Paper

- Recycle junk mail, inserts, newspapers, and magazines when you have finished with them.
- Do not recycle paper that includes plastic or shiny foil.

Glass

- Wash out old bottles and jars before you recycle them.
- Do not recycle flat glass, such as broken mirrors or picture glass.

Cans

- Rinse out old cans and tins before you recycle them.
- Remove labels from the tins and recycle the paper.
- Squash tins and cans to make them flat before putting them into the recycling bin.

Plastic bottles

- Remove the tops of the plastic bottles and throw them away. The tops cannot be recycled.
- Squash plastic bottles to make them flat.

Glossary

aluminium silvery metal that is very light but very strong

archaeologist person who studies past cultures by digging up ancient artefacts and bones

canal channel dug through the land and filled with water, which is used to transport goods or for irrigation

cancer serious illness caused by a tumour (growth) in part of the body

cargo goods that are carried by a ship, truck, or aircraft

charity shop shop that sells second-hand clothes, books, and other goods to raise money for a particular charity

compost soil that contains the rotted remains of living things

container ship ship that carries cargo in large boxes called containers

current stream of moving water

developed country rich country

developing country poor country

engineer person who designs and maintains engines and other machinery, bridges, roads, and other manufactured items

furnace chamber in which heat is produced for a specific purpose

generate to produce

giftwrap paper that is used to wrap up presents

incinerator special container with a hot fire that burns rubbish

landfill site place where rubbish is dumped and buried

litter rubbish that is dropped on the ground or in a river or the sea instead of being thrown into a bin

local council group of people who run the services of an area. It is responsible for recycling and rubbish collection, among other activities.

magnet any substance that attracts iron and steel

methane gas made up of carbon and hydrogen. Methane is produced when living things rot. Methane burns well and can be used as a fuel.

microbe tiny living thing, such as a bacterium or another germ

organic substance that contains carbon and comes from a living thing

packaging container or wrapper that something is sold in

paper mill factory that produces paper from wood pulp

pollute to make dirty

process to change something by treating it in a particular way

quarry place where stone is dug or blasted out of the ground

recycling processing paper, glass, and other materials so that they can be used again

sewage waste water from baths, sinks, and toilets

shrink-wrapped packaging in which an object is wrapped in plastic and then the plastic is shrunk to fit tightly around the object

transit journey of goods and people from place to place

translucent cloudy but not see-through

wormery self-contained system for producing compost using worms that break down kitchen waste

Find out more

Books

Recycling (Go Facts Environmental Issues), Ian Rohr (A & C Black Publishers Ltd, 2007)

Recycling (Your Environment), Jen Green (Franklin Watts, 2007)

Rubbish Disposal (Action for the Environment), D. Jackson Bedford (Franklin Watts, 2006)

Waste and Recycling (Green Files), Steve Parker (Heinemann Library, 2004)

Waste and Recycling (Helping our Planet), Sally Morgan (Evans Brothers Ltd, 2008)

Waste, Recycling and Reuse (Sustainable Futures), Sally Morgan (Evans Brothers Ltd, 2005)

Websites

This website includes lots of information about recycling different things, from aluminium and tin to paper and plastic. There are also some fun facts and exciting games to play:
www.ecy.wa.gov/programs/swfa/kidspage/

Another great website that tells you all about waste and recycling and what you can do to help. The site includes lots of fun games and online activities:
www.recyclezone.org.uk/

Meet Ollie and his friends at this fun website about recycling. You can enter competitions, have your own say, and find out more about reducing, reusing, and recycling:
www.olliesworld.com/uk/

Index